If Two Agree

By Bill and Nate Johnson

As told to Clair Verway

Again, truly I tell you that if two of you on earth agree about anything they ask for, it will be done for them by my Father in heaven. (Matthew 18:19 NIV)

CONTENTS

FORWARD

I first met Nate Johnson shortly after he was released from prison. I was a youth pastor at Bridge Bible Church in Muskegon at the time, and I founded an outreach organization called Bridge to Communities. Talking with Nate convinced us that there was a critical need to help people coming to Muskegon after being released from prison. Nate joined our board and shared in our outreach efforts. In 2014, we initiated a partnership with a reentry organization in Holland, Michigan. After an unprecedented season of growth, we became independent and known as Fresh Coast Alliance. Today, we serve adult men and women in reentry and recovery through Muskegon County.

I realized early on that Nate and I complemented each other. Nate is a walking embodiment of passion for reentry and recovery. He is great in front of a crowd and has real credibility because of his street experience and having been inside. My strengths are in administration and organization, so we work very well together. From the beginning, as I figured out how to grow and scale the ministry, Nate has continued to remind us to listen to the voices that are closest to the problem because they are also closest to the solutions. I am honored to partner with Nate to help men and women become successful in recovery or reentry and help them find hope in Jesus.

Joe Whalen, Executive Director,
Fresh Coast Alliance

If Two Agree

Chapter One

The young man sat on the bank of the Ohio River in Van Dyke Park watching the lights of a 15-barge tow slowly slide under the Big Four Bridge in the glow of the western sky. The breeze brought him the scent of muddy river funk and diesel fumes. It wasn't necessarily a pleasant smell, but it was comforting because it was a contrast to the smells back at the house on Walnut street where he lived with his parents and five siblings. The walk to the river was his way of escape.

His father worked hard to provide for his family, but as a result, his parenting suffered. He wasn't abusive with his children or his wife, he was just not there. His wife wasn't really prepared to raise six kids either, so the young man went to the river to dream of better things. He didn't know that what he was looking for, but he knew something was missing. As he grew up, he grew restless, and the river was symbolic of moving on, moving away.

There wasn't much of interest to a teenage boy in an Indiana river town in 1968. When Bill thought about what life held for him after graduation from Clarksville High School, his thoughts were always about getting out of town. Its location on the Ohio River had allowed Jeffersonville Boat & Machine Company to become the largest inland shipbuilder in the country, but Bill was more interested in what lay downriver than whatever Jeffboat had to offer.

Bill enjoyed school and couldn't understand why some of his friends wanted to skip out as often as they could. He loved the cop shows on TV and dreamed of becoming a special agent like Lewis Erskine on *The F.B.I.* When Bill graduated, he enrolled at Indiana University with plans to study criminal justice in preparation for application to the F.B.I. He even had an interview scheduled with the agency.

Unfortunately, it wasn't long before Bill got lured into the sex, drugs and rock-and-roll that was so prevalent in the 60's. Quickly, getting high became more interesting that getting hired. He never went to the interview with the F.B.I. Instead, he moved to the Indiana University campus in Bloomington, Indiana where the hippie counter-culture was in full swing.

In the wee hours of one morning, Bill returned to his room to be met by campus security and local police. He had several illegal substances on his person, and he was immediately arrested. He was taken to jail where he sat for a couple days. Bill's friends at IU heard that he got busted, so they pooled their money and posted his bond. After Bill got out, he continued doing what he had been doing before the arrest. Because he needed money for a lawyer, Bill did the only thing he could think of: he secured a large amount of LSD for resale. This pattern would be repeated time and again.

The case didn't result in any jail time for Bill, so he went ahead with plans to return home for a short visit and then head for New Jersey to connect with some people he met at IU who promised to hook him up if he came out. They lived in a motel room for the summer, engaging in all the activities of the drug subculture there. He went partly because he wanted to continue his experiments with the various drugs that were being used. The other reason he went East instead of back to Jeffersonville was because he had gotten a girl pregnant and didn't want to face the consequences.

One morning in August while they were all asleep,

his girlfriend from Jeffersonville showed up at the motel room. Surprise! She was several months pregnant with Bill's child. At fourteen, Bill had fathered a child who was given up for adoption. The stigma attached to having children born out of wedlock was too much this time. Bill knew this would never be acceptable to his family. After a couple weeks, he and his girlfriend made plans to return to Jeffersonville to get married. Sadly, back home in Indiana, his new wife also became addicted. In order to support this kind of habit, Bill turned to crime.

As often happens, Bill's experimentation with drugs led ultimately to heroin addiction, and that was his downfall. Once he got hooked, he needed a fix every four to six hours, and that got expensive. Of necessity, Bill turned to crime. It worked for a short time, but eventually his luck ran out and he was arrested for robbery and assault. His conviction resulted in a prison sentence of ten years. Strange as it may sound, when the jail door closed on him, Bill felt a sense of relief. The vicious treadmill of drug addiction had run him ragged, and he was glad for the relief, even though he suffered wicked withdrawal symptoms from the sudden end to his drugs.

Chapter Two

That young man in the jail cell was me, Bill Johnson, Kentucky Department of Corrections number 30629. At this point in my life, the department of corrections had not corrected much in my life. Once I learned how to navigate prison ways, life inside wasn't that much different from life in the streets. I ran afoul of the system often enough that I was labeled incorrigible and transferred to Eddyville, Kentucky's only maximum-security prison. Even there I got by pretty well, but something was happening inside of me. Looking back, I know it was the Spirit of God beginning His work in me, softening my heart in subtle ways.

The biggest thing I remember is how I started to feel genuine concern for my wife's situation. When I got locked up, my wife was still struggling with her addition. I began to wonder if she was doing alright. I began to think that if there was a god out there somewhere, maybe he would help my wife if I prayed for her. Every night before I went to sleep, I prayed. I thought of it as sort of a test to see if God really existed. I figured if he answered my prayers, I would know he was real. If nothing happened, it would confirm my suspicions that everything about God and church and the Bible was just another scam.

One evening about a month after I had begun to pray, a letter was pushed under the door of my cell. When I saw that it was from my wife, it was like a light came on in my head. I knew instantly that God really does exist, and he hears our prayers. In the letter, my wife told me she had entered a drug rehabilitation program in Michigan called Teen Challenge. To my surprise, she said she had received Christ as her Lord and Savior. I was glad to know she was alright, but I didn't know what to make of her newfound faith in God. It certainly didn't occur to me that there might be something in that for me.

For many days after the letter arrived, I walked the loop on the exercise yard with the Holy Spirit continuously whispering in my ear "What about you?" At that point I wasn't really interested in God or in changing anything about my life. I realized that in a few more months, it was time for me to go before the parole board. The reality of facing the parole board began to settle in on me like a kind of dark mist. As I pondered what was about to happen, I was struck with the realization that I had not one positive thing to show the parole board that might convince them that I was at least attempting rehabilitation on some level.

Not only was there nothing good to show them, I continued to have run-ins on the inside. The reason I was sent to Eddyville was because of my unwillingness to go along with the program. My rap sheet was extensive: charges for forgery, burglary, carrying a concealed deadly weapon, armed robbery, along with indictments in three states for trafficking in narcotics. None of that would look good to a parole board. I began scurrying around trying to find some available program within the prison that I could join to give me something positive to show to the board. I soon discovered that I had waited too long to do so. Those doors were closed to me.

I remembered one of the guys I had known in Kentucky State Reformatory was involved in the chapel program in Eddyville. It seemed like he was a different person from the one I knew from before. I sought him out and asked if there was anything available within the chapel that I could connect with. After a couple days he told me there was counseling available by volunteers from the outside. He made me an appointment for me which gave me a ray of hope.

When the day of my appointment came, I made my way up to the counseling center on the second floor of the chapel. As I stood outside the room waiting for my turn, I could see two middle-aged women through the large glass windows seated at the counseling table with two inmates. One of the counselors made eye contact. Instead of fear, as you would expect, I saw something I don't recall having ever seen before. Even though I couldn't define it at the time, I came to know I was looking into the eyes of love: the fiery, reckless love of God that He had for me personally. Somehow, I knew that what I was seeing was the very thing that I had always been looking for since my days in back home in Jeffersonville.

When my turn came to meet the counselor, I was introduced to the woman whose look had communicated God's love to me. Marinell shared the plan of salvation with me almost immediately. After listening to her for only a few minutes, I agreed to pray the sinner's prayer. I didn't know everything that meant at the time, but it began the most important journey of my life.

I first met Marinell in February, and my parole hearing was only three months away. We continued to meet on a weekly basis as she shared the Word of God and told me about her own experience as a follower of Christ. Even though my original motivation to meet with a counselor was to look good to the parole board, this soon became secondary to me. I determined that because I was a follower of Christ, I would not lie to the parole board even when they asked the hard questions.

I began to devour the Word of God. I discovered that God intended for His followers to share Him with other people who didn't know Him. I was a bit fearful at first, mostly because I didn't know how to go about it. I began to pray that God would arrange an opportunity for me to do so. It wasn't long before I was in conversation with another inmate that I didn't know very well. I knew on the inside of me that God had arranged this meeting. We talked for hours about religion, God, and many other things. I was able to share with him my own experience of coming to know God as my Savior and about being born again.

After our talk, we went our separate ways. Later that afternoon, word began to circulate that someone had just been killed in the gym. I soon learned that the man who was killed was the guy that I had talked with earlier about eternity, heaven and hell, God and salvation. It affected me deeply to think that the man I had spoken to only hours before was now in the presence of God, his eternal destiny in the balance. I was struck by the necessity to share the gospel with anyone I could because life is so fragile, especially in prison. That urgency remains with me to this day.

When the day for my parole hearing came, I told the truth about everything they asked. As I walked out of the room, the enemy screamed in my ear, "You idiot! You just told them everything! You're not going anywhere." The following minutes seemed like an eternity until I was called back in to receive the parole board's judgment. After asking me about a couple other things from my past, they gave me their determination. I'll never forget their words. "Mr. Johnson, we have learned from experience that the only people who ever get out these places and stay out are those who have had a genuine born-again experience. We believe that you've had one, and because of that we have made a unanimous decision to grant you a parole." On July 31, 1977, I walked out of prison.

Chapter Three

The kid was barely 18 when his life took a dramatic turn. He knew more about survival on the streets than many men much older. He learned early that he could buy dope from a dealer and sell it for double what he paid. The money he could make slinging drugs was for more than his job washing dishes at Mike's Cro would ever make him. His older brother turned him on to that fact of life while he was still attending Bunker Junior High. He worked his way up from $5 buys to much, much more. At 18, he was a major player in the Mason Street Mafia in Muskegon.

Nate had already had some minor beefs with the law, but he felt as if he was invincible, like most teens. He had been busted a few times, but that only lent to his street cred with the gangs. The friction was building with the guys from the Wood Street neighborhood. Things came to a head when Nate's buddy, Tyjuan, said the Wood Street guys were going to beat him up after school because he had been seen talking to one of their girls. The Mafia hit the Wood Street gang pretty hard that day by overpowering them three to one. They felt like their territory was secure, but that was the beginning of the gang wars in Muskegon. The young men started to gather in their own neighborhood gangs: the Jackson Hill Black Gangsters who had been around for quite some time, the AVP (Amityville Players), the Pine Street crew who called themselves 911, and the South Side Hustlers. This created territorial divisions in the city.

In October of 1998, some Wood Street guys were flexing at a Big Reds game, but the police were there so nothing happened immediately. After the game, some of the Mafia got into a fight with the Wood Street guys at a club. Nate and a few others had stayed in the neighborhood to do some business. Late in the evening, one of their gang stopped by to inform them about the fight at the club. He told them that things were going to escalate as they often did, so he passed them a .32 caliber pistol.

That night in the wee hours, Nate and a buddy, Goldie, went to the Shell station to cop some munchies. On their way there, they heard a gunshot and realized that something was going down in the neighborhood. When they got back from the store, an older guy named Chip accused them of shooting at his cousin's car and almost killing him. Of course, they had a suspicion that the

.32 may have been involved, but they didn't know for sure, so they played dumb.

When Nate's best friend, Ted, came and told them that they did shoot at the car, things got complicated. Ted told Chip that the car they were in was the same one the Wood Street guys were borrowing from a dope dealer and cruising around town in. They thought it was them out looking for trouble. Nate and his buddies sat down on the porch of an abandoned house to figure out how to handle the situation. They knew Chip was still pissed, so they were debating whether to jump him and settle the issue.

Nate suddenly noticed that there was a car pulling off a side street and heading their way. The car rolled by slowly but didn't stop. Once it got to the next intersection, it made a left and rolled on slowly. Nate figured out these must be the Wood Street guys looking for their target. He later learned that in fact, Chip was the one who beat up the Wood Street guy at the club. After the car had rolled by them, Chip and Ted went back to arguing in the street. Nate and Goldie went back to the porch.

A minute later, Nate realized that the car had circled back and was coming up the alley. He warned Ted and Chip to get out of the street. Before they could move, shots rang out and everybody headed for cover behind the house. Nate and Ted were going toward the alley beside the house when they began to hear slugs banging into the siding around them. They dived for cover as the vehicle sped away. When Nate tried to get Ted to move to a safer position, Ted didn't respond. Finally, Nate realized that Ted had been shot. He wasn't getting up again.

After the vehicle was gone, Chip came back to see what happened to the two younger men. He tried to help Nate get Ted up, but it was clear that he was mortally wounded. Nate begged him to go to a house for help, but no one would open their door at that hour, especially after hearing gun shots. Finally, Nate ran down the block to a friend's house and roused someone. He told them to call the police; then he ran back to where Ted lay. Chip suggested that they try to make sure there was nothing incriminating on Ted, so they went through his pockets. They pulled some drugs out of his pockets and found the .32 on him, so Nate threw it as hard as he could into the next yard. That would prove to be a mistake.

Nate had not grown up in the seamy underworld of Muskegon. In his early years, he attended a Christian elementary school and his father was a pastor. Until he was thirteen his life revolved around school and church activities. Then something happened. His dad called him and his older brother, Eli, to the basement one day for a talk. Nate wasn't sure what to expect, but Eli had been kicked out of the Christian school a short time before, and he suspected it was related somehow. He could never have imagined what he was about to be told.

It was obvious that his dad was struggling to get out what he wanted to say. When it finally came out, Nate couldn't believe his ears. His dad shared that in his younger years he had been addicted to narcotics, had been arrested, and had spent several years in prison. His dad explained that after he came to the Lord, he turned away from his former life and reconciled with his wife, the boys' mom, and began his new life as a pastor. Nate could see that his dad's heart was breaking because Eli was starting to head down the same path. His dad cautioned the boys not to be lured into the life of the streets no matter how exciting it may seem. He was telling them about his failures in hopes they would not make the same mistakes.

Their father's words had the opposite of the desired effect on the two boys. They thought it was so cool that their dad had real street cred. It made them want to be like their dad in all the wrong ways.

When Nate reached the fifth grade, he asked to be allowed to go to public school instead of the Christian school. Knowing it was a fight that they couldn't win, Nate's mom and dad agreed. Forcing Nate to stay in Christian school would only make him more rebellious than he already was. Sadly, in the public school, there was no influence working to keep Nate from getting deeper into the wrong life-style. And he got in deep.

At fifteen, Nate began selling weed. Soon he realized that crack cocaine had a much higher profit potential, so he moved up in the business. To make money to purchase his inventory, Nate began stealing and selling whatever he could. He had been stealing cars for joy rides, so now he began to find rides with expensive sound equipment he could sell. It was grand theft auto that got him his first serious time: thirty days in Muskegon County Jail plus the time he spent awaiting trial. It was an easy bit for the street-wise kid, so when he got out, it was back to business as usual. For a while.

Chapter Four

When I was released from the Kentucky Department of Corrections, I had three days to go home, visit family, and make my way to Grand Haven, Michigan to report to my parole agent. After living and working in Grand Haven alone for a couple months, my wife arrived. After being estranged for more than four years without any contact at all here we were back together again. Curiously, we both had come to Christ a single month apart. To me it was obvious that it was God who had brought us back together. I was sure that everything would continue to unfold in a miraculous way. Little did I know how needy and unprepared we both were to attempt to live together in a marriage relationship.

What I did know (I thought) was how ready I was to do great things for God. I had read and studied the Bible seriously while incarcerated, and I had memorized a lot of scripture. I believed God had anointed me to teach the Word of God. When we would get together with other believers, they recognized the anointing upon my life to communicate the Word of God. Because I had memorized so much Scripture, I also recognized that that gave me an advantage a lot of other believers didn't have. Ministry became everything to me. It came before everything, including my family. At this time, we only had our firstborn son Yosef, who was about 8 years old. What I realize now that I didn't then was that I was drawing my identity from doing ministry. I also sought acceptance from God by doing ministry. This is a common problem in the body of Christ today. I based everything in my life on my performance.

Needless to say, this was a train wreck waiting to happen. The crazy thing was that at the same time, more and more people were beginning to gravitate toward us when we would gather to fellowship with other believers and to share the Word. We never intended to plant a church. The best way to describe what took place was that a church began to emerge around us. Because of the anointing upon my life, others would look to me for spiritual direction. Even though deep inside I knew I wasn't called to be a pastor, others began to relate to me that way. I finally concluded that must be what I am.

Again, in all of this I was driven internally by the desire for acceptance, identity, and affirmation. After a few years of living in Grand Haven we moved to Muskegon where most of the people we were interacting with lived. I also convinced myself that God was calling me to leave my job and go into fulltime ministry. It wasn't God; it was me, but that's what I did. Eli was born in 1979 and Nathan was born in 1981 a week or so before we made the move to Muskegon. His younger sister, Bethany, was born in Muskegon in 1983.

As I said, I put ministry before everything, including family in an attempt to meet the deep needs of my own starving soul. I had no idea what it meant to be a husband and how to love my wife. I didn't know how to give and receive love. Having grown up without any love or discipline and having read in the Bible about child discipline, I thought that was all that was needed. I had heard somewhere that "rules without relationship produce rebellion;" that was proving out to be true

As the saying goes "hindsight is 20/20". As I look back at the time between when my wife and I first came back together until the time that we actually divorced, I can now clearly see why our marriage and family life didn't have much of a chance of succeeding. The best way to describe my relationship with my wife is we were like two ticks and no dog.

I've had to do some major rethinking about my

theology concerning who God is and how life works. One of the realities I discovered was that even though something may be the will of God, and it may be part of your destiny, it isn't automatic. I still believe that it was the will of God for my relationship with my wife to be restored and for our family together to prosper. I truly thought that if I just stayed in the marriage and held on, God would make it work out and we would all live happily ever after. I now realize that as long as there is a human will (or two) involved, there will always be a chance for failure simply because God in His goodness will never violate our human will and force to behave a certain way.

Let me say we had a whole grocery list of reasons why our marriage and home life failed so miserably. I had absolutely no idea what it meant to be a husband and very little idea what it meant to be a father. I truly didn't know what it meant to love another person or to be loved. By the time I could see that I was a major part of the problem, it was too late for our marriage to recover. Except for an act of divine intervention our marriage was doomed. There was no act of divine intervention, at least not one that I could discern at the time. I continued to believe that as long as I stayed on the ship, God would somehow step in and save us, even if that meant He did so even as the ship was sinking beneath the surface of turbulent waters. It didn't happen.

I remember waking up one morning, sitting on the edge of the bed, and realizing that this ship was not going to be rescued. I knew it was over. One of the things that kept me in my marriage through those years was the false belief that the call of God on my life would be rendered null and void if I were to become divorced. That was bad enough, but I also believed that if I were to divorce, not only would I be rejected in ministry, but I would no longer be acceptable to God as a person. I believed that no matter what I did with the rest of my life, I would be a failure when I stood before God in the judgment. As you might imagine this created problems for me on the inside.

Even though I was willing to stay in the marriage for the sake of the call, there was nothing I could do to prevent a divorce from happening. I felt trapped; I felt betrayed in the worst way. It was a hard pill to swallow. The God who saved me and demanded that I stay in the marriage was not going to save my marriage after all. I can't describe how hurt and how betrayed I felt. It was like being the brunt of a really bad joke.

I knew that I would have to step down from the church leadership as the lead pastor and walk away from the only thing that I believed could provide me with security, acceptance and purpose. I continued going through the motions, at least for a while. We left the church and wandered from place to place for a time. I was numb inside, unable to reconcile what was happening to me with a God who said He loved me. I was deeply hurt and offended at God. I quit praying and reading the Word. What would be the point?

Another lesson is to be learned here. Because I had withdrawn from the Lord internally, even though I was unaware of it, my heart was becoming hardened. It took several years of neglect and holding onto the offense internally before the garden of my heart became overgrown with thistles. Its surface was covered with nettles, and its stone wall was broken down (see Proverbs 24:30-34). The heart is truly like a garden. When we neglect it, and we no longer cultivate and care for it, it returns to its natural state just like uncultivated soil; it becomes hard and unyielding.

The hardening didn't happen overnight. Little by little, day after day surely my heart became fallow, hard and unyielding. Trying to do life without God is pride. "The arrogance of your heart has deceived you." (Obadiah 1:3) It took several years for my heart to become completely fallow. When It did, I was ready to descend into the "far country". (Luke 15:13) I never in a million years would have thought that I would end up back in the place that God had once saved me out of.

I can look back now and see how the enemy had meticulously arranged things to make it easy for me to return to the life I once turned my back on to follow Jesus. I realized that there was nothing left inside. I was dazed, disillusioned, and deeply disappointed. I was wearing a blanket of betrayal. I don't know if there are words to describe the depth to which I was wounded. It was more than I could process. Just as the disciples returned to the only life they had ever known after the heart-shattering disappointment of the crucifixion, I returned to life in the streets after my divorce became inevitable.

I wish I had never told my boys about my former life. The idea backfired in a big way. My sons, Eli and Nate, were deeply involved in the drug scene in Muskegon. My wife, Brenda, began to break under the strain and started to use narcotics again. I began to doubt the genuineness of my call to ministry.

After I had given my all to follow after God and answer the call He had placed on my life, I found that the One who could have prevented this tragedy didn't. It was like a catch 22. I was sure that God had called me into ministry, but my theology at the time would not permit me to continue in ministry and be divorced. In my mind, it seemed my existence would now be without purpose. The One who called me knew what the outcome of my marriage would be; He had the ability to save it, but He didn't. I felt as though I was condemned to a meaningless existence.

I wasn't mad at God, but I was deeply hurt by what seemed like His betrayal. It was only later that the disappointment turned to offense. I became offended at God. That day marked the beginning of my descent back into Egypt. I didn't make a rational decision to quit pursuing God; I just did. I no longer prayed, no longer read the Word, no longer desired to fellowship with other believers. I continued to work and do the bare minimum to keep things afloat, at least outwardly. I lived on my own little island of despair.

For the next couple of years, my heart was growing cold and hard, but I did not know it. With the divorce looming, I knew that I was going to need finances that I did not presently have. After wrestling with what to do, I made the decision to purchase a quantity of crack cocaine to sell. I thought I would be safe handling it since cocaine was never my thing. I made the arrangements to travel to my hometown to pick up the product. Crack cocaine came into existence after I had left the drug scene back in the 70's, so I had never tried it. I felt I should try the product to make sure it was what it was reported to be. I did, and that was a huge mistake.

Because of the hardness of my heart and the inner pain and turmoil I was experiencing, the drug offered a welcome relief and diversion from the painful struggle raging in my heart. Given my propensity to addiction, the result was inevitable. It wasn't long before the drugs that I had purchased to resell were consumed. At first, I attempted to keep my drywall business going. It didn't take long before I abandoned the business to pursue the high and the temporary relief that it afforded.

In no time, I drained my accounts and quit paying any bills. I was thoroughly trapped in the clutches of addiction. I had numerous credit cards with generous limits left. I also began to use heroin. I was consuming copious amounts of both drugs. This insanity continued for about six months. Eventually I was arrested in Grand Haven for possession of cocaine. Around the time of my arrest, the money had just about run out. I had gone through approximately $152,000 in six months. Things were about to drastically change.

Even though the money ran out, the voracious appetite for the drugs didn't. I had to come up with a plan. I gave no thought to getting involved in a recovery program. There was nothing to recover for. I didn't want to return to armed robbery because of the long sentence if I were caught. The safest way I knew to acquire money without working was shoplifting and then resale. I began to do this, and things deteriorated. I ended up staying with people who were also using. I was living in the unfinished basement of a crack house, sleeping on an old box spring covered with a discarded blanket.

One night, Eli came over with a package of the powdered cocaine that he was selling. Earlier in the evening he had a run-in with someone over drugs. The guy followed Eli and brought two friends with him. The three men burst into the house, and while the two kept me at bay, the other guy took the drugs from Eli.

After they were gone, we went and found Nate. From there we picked up a gun and went looking for the three men. All I could think of while we were driving and looking for these guys was if we get pulled over and I'm found with a gun, I'm in trouble. If we find the three guys and someone ends up dead as a result, things really will get difficult. Thank God, neither happened.

Chapter Five

When Nate and the guys heard sirens coming, they ran between houses and down alleys to Ted's house. After they told his mom Ted had been shot, she was hysterical. They all headed back to the scene, which by then was surrounded by police cars and yellow crime-scene tape. They tried to blend in with the crowd that had gathered, but soon the detectives were scouring the neighborhood for anyone with information. They eventually caught up with Nate and took him to the police station for questioning.

Nate tried to make up a plausible story that had the ring of truth but left him out of the shooting. He mentioned the walk to the store and calling the girls. He tried to convince the police that he and Goldie had come upon the scene after the shooting was over. What Nate couldn't know was that the police were about to hear three different stories that did not line up with his. First, Ted's mom would identify him as the person who told her about Ted's death. Second, the girls were afraid they would be dragged in because they had been in the area at the time, so they identified the principal players, Nate included. Finally, the driver of the car was the son of a department of corrections investigator, so he got scared and told his mom. She turned him in, and he became State's evidence. Nate was trapped before he knew what hit him.

Miraculously, there were no serious charges against Nate related to the shooting. After he copped to the true story (almost: he failed to mention the gun), he was set free. When they couldn't find the gun, they told Nate he would be held for obstruction of justice if he didn't come clean and tell them where the gun was. Truly, Nate had no idea since he had thrown it wildly into the night. He was also afraid that the gun might be traced back to some other incident he or his buddies had been involved in, so he was not anxious for it to be found.

For two more years, Nate continued to live the Mason Street Mafia life. Then, to no one's surprise, Nate was caught and charged with delivery of cocaine. He spent his time, then went back to business. Then, Nate committed armed robbery in May of 2000, but the charges were dropped because no one cooperated with the police. He soon caught another beef for which he spent four months on tether. In October 2000, he got off tether, then went back to business until he was caught for delivery of cocaine, armed robbery, and a felony firearm charge in November. After skating on the earlier charges in May, the judge warned Nate that if he ever appeared before him again, he would send him to prison. Period. End of freedom. The time had come. The judge sentenced Nate to five to twenty years in the Michigan Department of Corrections.

So Nate was finally got sent into the hands of the MDOC. After being assessed in Riverside Correctional Facility in Ionia, he was classified as a level four, the highest level of security known as maximum security. He was sent to St. Louis Correctional Facility where he got his first taste of what prison really meant. Razor wire, multiple gates and a prison atmosphere like you see in the movies. Only this was for real. For many years to come.

That was me, Nate Johnson. I was clueless to a lot of the dysfunction going on in our family. It wasn't until I was in my early teens that I discovered that we were a bit different as a family. Like anything, if you don't have something else to base your experience on, then to you it's normal until something different comes along. I don't want to imply our upbringing was the worst, because it was not. I have met people who have had worse conditions growing up than ours.

As a youngster I could always remember looking up to my dad and wanting to be like him. My earliest memories of my mom were filled with love. I remember she was an aerobics instructor at the YMCA. Before I started kindergarten, I would have to go with her, sit in the corner of the room, and play with my coloring book or watch a bunch of ladies jump around to music playing on my mother's big boom box. Mom was always well liked, and it seemed like she knew everyone. She was in good shape and very attractive. And she talked a lot. We kids would always hate it when she would get into a conversation somewhere away from home because we knew that this was going to turn into a one-hour sermon.

Both of my parents pastored a church together and from my standpoint they were both leaders. It seemed that everyone looked up to them. I remember mom taking the women from the church to Indiana to my Gramma Nell's house for women's retreats. She was really outgoing and was kind of the life of the party.

Dad, on the other hand, I remember being more laid back. He was the pastor of a local church in

Muskegon called Faith Fellowship Assembly. A lot of people looked up to him. I remember on Sunday mornings Dad would get to the church early before everyone else. He always took this big briefcase with a bunch of paperwork in it. In my attempt to be like him I begged him to get me one like it. One day we went to the Goodwill and he bought me a used suitcase. I remember bringing it home and going down into the basement where dad had his office and filling it up with old books from his book shelves thinking to myself, "Man, I feel important." I couldn't wait until Sunday's came around so that I could take it with me. That excitement lasted about two Sunday's and then everything was back to normal.

I remember one afternoon when I was about 11 years old my dad taking me and my brother Eli down into the basement of our house saying that he wanted to talk with us. He saw that we were beginning to head in the wrong direction. I had been caught stealing at the local Plumb's store by the floor walker while attempting to get out of the store with chewing tobacco. The scary thing was that stealing almost became like a sport to us. We would steal in all most every store we entered.

When we got to the family room in the basement

we sat on the floor and dad pulled out an old scrap book. It had pictures of Mom and Dad when they were younger, and it had newspaper clippings of them. As Dad began to explain what we were looking at, he told us for the first time that he had been to prison. I was shocked, I was amazed. When we asked what he was in prison for he told us for armed robbery. We couldn't believe it; we thought that it was so cool and wondered how many guys could actually say that their Dad had been to prison.

I know in dad's mind he was probably thinking that if he told us this part of his past that it would have a profound effect on us and encourage us not to continue doing what we were doing. In fact, it caused us to look at our dad as someone who was automatically a tough guy because he had been to prison. We read all the newspaper clippings that he had kept of crimes that he had committed.

At the beginning of '93 while I was in 5th grade, Dad felt led to step down from pastoring Faith Fellowship. At this time, things were getting a bit out of control at home. Mom and Dad were doing a lot more arguing; my brother and I were being pulled towards the streets, and my little sister Bethany was caught up in the rapture of everything going on. I had already been caught shoplifting from the grocery store and Dad could sense that things were going in the wrong direction.

I didn't realize that my Mother had become addicted to pills. Mother had served time in prison just like Dad, and both of them had been addicted to heroin. Shortly after Mom was released from prison she had moved to Muskegon, Michigan to enter the Teen Challenge program. One of my parent's friends from back home in Southern Indiana had gotten clean and given his life to the Lord while he was in prison. He came to Teen Challenge first. My mother came some time during the year of 1976 with Dad to follow in '77 when he was released from KDOC.

After Mom and Dad were reunited and had been in Michigan for about 5 years', Mom had begun taking pills again, but this time it was slightly more legitimate. Mom had hurt her back and my grandmother was sending her pills that had prescribed for her. Eventually this led to Mom finding a doctor who would write her a prescription to pain pills. The addiction that had been dormant was being resurrected.

After Dad stepped down from leading the church you could tell that something shifted in our home.

We wandered from church to church for about a year, but nothing seemed to fit and eventually we just stopped going to church all together.

In the summer of '93, I expressed my interest in leaving the Christian school so that I could go to school with my brother and friends at the local junior high. When I asked him, I really did not think that he would say yes, but he did. I remember my heart skipped a beat with excitement.

A year earlier my brother had gotten expelled from the Christian school and was sent to the public school. He always told to me that he liked it a lot better than the private school that we had attended. I was so excited when I let my friends in the neighborhood know that I would be at school with them the following school year.

This was the same year that I caught my first criminal case: Reckless Use of a Firearm. As the years went on my involvement with the streets began to increase. We had upped our stealing from local stores and gas stations to stealing from houses and stealing appliances that we could sell for money. My criminal career had only just begun.

Chapter Six

I finally realized that I had come to the end of my self. I realized I had made a mess of everything good that had ever come my way. By this time, my son Eli had died from a drug overdose. My daughter, Bethany was Bethany was beginning to get in trouble of her own including legal trouble for stealing a car. She was placed in Boys Town by the courts for a year. My estranged wife was still struggling with her addiction. Nate was serving time for robbery and drug charges in a maximum-security prison. As often happens when someone realizes there is nothing left for him to do, I began to pray.

Through the experience of my own recovery, I learned how utterly weak and incapable I was of running my own life. Being brought to the end of myself – very much aware of my own spiritual bankruptcy – and coming to grips with the fact that it was impossible for life to work without God. There was no longer any question that it all depended upon Him. Even as I write this, I'm reminded of the verse in Jer.17:14 that reads: "Heal me, O Lord, and I will be healed; Save me and *will be saved, For Thou art my praise*." There was nothing left inside to even want to try to save myself.

Because of my own experience, I was convinced that the same was true concerning my son Nate. I knew what it was like to be where he was, to have a heart that was hardened through sin and that only God would be able to break through that hardness and reach him on the inside. I knew there was nothing that I or anyone else could do or say that would cause him to turn around. The good part of losing all hope in the flesh is that it becomes easy to believe and trust in the One who is able.

I decided to contact a couple who had been a part of the church family that I had pastored years earlier. Although I had gotten my heart right before God, I was still in desperate need of fellowship of other believers. I had no desire to return to church, at least not church as usual. The reason I called the couple was I knew that Mary had the gift of mercy, and I knew that I would be met with open arms, acceptance and love. After catching up on our lives, we realized that we shared a common concern for our children. They introduced me to their neighbor, and I found that they also had a son who was recently incarcerated. Since we all a concern for our children, we decided to begin meeting together for the purpose of praying for our children.

For the next two or three years we met together every week and prayed accordingly. Lest you think it was our great praying that caused God to intervene, let me assure you otherwise. None of us had an exceptional prayer life. We had long periods of no prayer, and dry and uneventful prayers. In retrospect, it's easy to see that it was the persistence of our praying that moved God into action. I'm convinced it was simply because we kept praying. The key is revealed in Galatians 6:9 "And let us not lose heart in doing good (praying) for in due time we shall reap if we do not grow weary" The key to obtaining every harvest is perseverance. (Luke 8:15)

Chapter Seven

The only books I had to read at Riverside were from something called Chaplain Ray's Prison Ministry. They were testimonials from guys who had surrendered to God while in prison and then gone on to do some powerful ministry when they got out. I wasn't really interested in them, but I was locked in my cell twenty-three hours a day on quarantine, so I began reading out of desperation. I know some seeds of thought were planted, but as soon as I rode out to the max prison in St. Louis, I went back to my old ways.

After two years of smoking weed and fighting and basically living a messed-up life, I began to wonder if there was something better. To my surprise, my appellate attorney showed up one day to inform me there was a technicality in my sentencing that might get me some time off my sentence. She warned me it was no sure thing, but if the judge wanted, he could reduce my time by up to five years. I know it sounds like those people you hear making bargains with God, but I told Him that if He could get the judge to cooperate, I would give the rest of my life to Him.

I began praying every day that God would intervene in my behalf. Several months later, my attorney argued my case before the judge, and it seemed like a miracle from God: he agreed to reduce my sentence from seventeen and a half to twelve and a half years. It may not seem like much, but I took that five years as a gift from God, and I renewed my commitment to do what I could to serve Him.

I began going to church and reading my Bible. I was still smoking cigarettes and talking trash, but I started to feel uncomfortable with my lifestyle. About then I heard a TV preacher talk about Judgment Day and having to give an account for everything I had done. It really got me thinking. Soon after that, I heard a sermon by T.D. Jakes talking about how God doesn't just use "good" people. He pointed out that Moses and David and even Paul were criminals in one sense of the word, but God sure used them.

The thing that really got me was when T.D. Jakes said, "The next ten years of your life, God is going to do a work on the inside of you." It hit me like he was talking directly to me: I had almost exactly ten years left on my sentence. I was sure Jakes was talking to me. That sermon started a war inside me. I wasn't really convinced that Christianity was the true religion. At that time, I thought it had been invented in America, so it didn't seem like it could be the real thing.

I finally realized that I would have to make a commitment of all or nothing. I came off the big yard one night and finally got real with God. I told Him I knew I was messed up, and I wanted Him to take my life and do whatever He wanted.

I remember the Holy Spirit saying almost immediately that I had stuff in my life that had to go. I took it literally and flushed my cigarettes, threw away my nasty rap music and just cleaned out my cell of anything that I thought was wrong. I went to sleep that night with a clean conscience for the first time since I was a kid.

During those ten years, God really was working in me. I read my Bible every chance I got. I just absorbed it like it was the best thing ever. I had the chance to pastor two different churches on the inside. I really identified with Moses in the way he spent forty years in the desert in Midian being prepared to lead God's people out of Egypt. I began to dream about what I would do when I got out.

When my time was served, I was able to move in with my Dad back in Muskegon. He had gotten his life cleaned up and had some connections that were really helpful. The best thing was taking me to a church where I met the girl of my dreams – literally. I had told God I wanted a truly sold-out Christian woman for my wife, and there she was, leading worship in the church my Dad went to. We began dating, and in no time, we were making plans to get married.

There were so many things that just fell into place when I came home that it is obvious God was doing it. I had a place to live; people gave me clothes and even a car. The perfect wife just walked into life like a movie script. Best of all, I met someone who was as passionate about ministry to ex-offenders as I was. Within a matter of months after getting out, I was doing what I know God had prepared for me to do.

Chapter Eight

If you are reading this book, there's a good chance that you have become discouraged, feel hopeless and trapped, or maybe you have given up all hope of anything good coming out of your personal life and circumstances. You may be unable to believe that there is still hope for other people and the other desperate situations around you. Perhaps it's because your children are getting worse instead of better. The problems have been going on so long that it seems beyond the possibility of repair.

Perhaps the problem is that your own life is in spiritual shambles. You believe you have not been a good parent. Perhaps things are where they are because of your own sin and folly. Maybe you have repented and are in a restored relationship to God, but there are still those consequences present because of past failure bad choices. Things appear hopeless and beyond any possible redemption. It really doesn't matter why you've given up.

Let me remind you that God is the God of impossible: His own Word declares Him to be the One "who gives life to the dead and calls into being that which does not exist." (Romans 4:17) And concerning Himself, He asks the question, "Is anything too hard for God?" (Jeremiah 32:27)

God's own testimony concerning the miracles, signs, and wonders He performed in Egypt in order to bring His people out of the "house of bondage". (Romans 9:17) He's the God of the impossible.

The salvation that God has provided for us is not limited to the forgiveness of sins and a guaranteed entrance into heaven when you die. The Greek word that is translated as salvation in the N.T. is a word with broad meaning. It speaks of saving, healing delivering in every area of life – body, soul, and spirit, the whole person. Our salvation begins with an act (being born again), but it continues as a process. God desires to save the whole person.

Salvation, from beginning to end, is provided by the grace of God, and is granted as a gift. It doesn't begin by grace and then get sustained by human performance. Because they don't understand this, many believers find themselves trapped in a performance-based salvation. Your right-standing with God is a gift. The only way that God will relate to you is through the medium of grace. If you work, He won't. If you quit working and instead trust Him, He'll work.

The point is that God loves you just like you are right now and not a future version of yourself. His salvation is perfect and available to all who call upon Him. The moment that you repent and believe He not only forgives your sins, but He remembers them no more. They are no longer on record in heaven as an offense. He promises that they will never be brought up again. That's good news!

The only reason Nate and I have shared our life story, warts and all, is because we want you to know that no one is beyond God's reach. I could have been completely discouraged and given up when Nate wound up in prison for the very same things that got me incarcerated. I know there were people on the outside praying for me when I was locked up. I also know that our prayers for Nate were instrumental in bringing him to the Lord.

So now about your children. We know from Scripture that God is concerned about individuals and their household. (Acts 16:33) We're told in 1 Cor.7:14 that our children are sanctified (set apart) unto God in a special way for salvation because of the faith of a parent who believes. In order to prepare yourself for the purpose of praying for your children, you begin by taking full responsibility for your past failures as a parent. Ask for, believe in, and receive His forgiveness for all you have done that would be displeasing to Him.

Once you've taken care of your unconfessed sin, you can begin to focus your attention on the matter of interceding for your children. You should begin collecting God's promises from His Word concerning our children. Remember that God loves it when you remind Him of what He has already spoken in His Word. The key is taking His word and turning it into your own personal dialogue with Him. We can use His word (promises) and turn them into believing prayer. It will be hard to miss when you base your prayers on the foundation of His own Word.

One reason why this is so effective is because of what we find written in 1 Jn.5:14-15. "And this is the confidence which we have before Him, that, if we ask anything according to His will, He hears us" "And if we know that He hears us in whatever we ask, we know that we have the requests that we have asked from Him." Since we know that His Word is His will, we can have confidence that He hears us and will answer us when we ask Him anything that is according to His word.

It will also be helpful to remember that Your salvation is a gift. (Ephesians 2:8-9) Your righteousness, your acceptance by Him, your access to His throne is all a gift from God's grace. The same way you received your salvation is how you maintain it. You were saved by grace; you must live by grace. You cannot maintain your salvation by your own works. (Colossians 2:6-7; Galatians 3:3)

You need to know that even though God could instantly answer your prayer and change your situation, He doesn't always work that way. The more common way that He works is through the process of time. There may be several reasons why He chooses to work this way, but I want to point you to just one. This reason can often be summed up in one word, and that word is relationship. God passionately desires a relationship with each one of His children.

One way in which that takes place is through the process of prayer. Remember that even though prayer can be an event, it is usually a process too. Remembering that will keep you from becoming discouraged along the way if things don't change immediately.

The best way to prepare your heart for intercession is to familiarize yourself with the promises of God that you intend to turn into prayer. Take time to meditate on each one; memorize them and carry them around in your heart. It may be helpful to look at the promises in some of the other Bible versions available. Once you've done that, you can now start your dialogue with God.

Here is an illustration of what that looks like. I always begin by thanking God for my children and I receive them as a gift from God (Psalm 127:3) (even though it may not always seem like they are). I thank Him for who He is to me. My God, my Father, My Savior, that he is kind, faithful and is not willing that any one perish, but that all come to repentance. One of my favorite verses for praying this way is in Job 33:14-18. When I use this Scripture for prayer, it will go something like this:

Father I ask you to fulfill your promise in Job 33:14-18. I ask you to speak to my son or my daughter (use their name) in the night seasons through dreams and visions. Open their ears during times like this. I ask You to seal up wisdom and Your instruction for salvation and all their needs in their hearts. Cause them to change their mind. I thank you that repentance is a gift from You. Cause your words to keep them from going into the ways of pride. Warn them of the eternal penalties of sin and keep them from the snares and traps that the enemy so readily sets for them. Please keep their feet from being taken. Thank you for hearing my prayer, thank you for answering my prayer. Thank you that you will do what you promised – in Your way and in Your time. Give me grace to continue to wait on you and stay believing. I thank you that not one word of all your great promises has ever failed!

Remember that prayer is intended to be a dialogue not a monologue. Always take time to listen to see what He may have to say to you. When He speaks, be sure to record it. Keep a journal specifically for this. Act on what He tells you when that's possible. Meditate and rehearse His promises and his words to you on a regular basis. By this you will be able to build yourself up in the Lord. Continue to bring this before the Lord until you know He has heard you (knowing in your inner man).

When that happens, your prayer needs to change. You then begin to thank Him for the answers that are already on the way. As you become familiar with this kind of praying, you can also incorporate other promises and combine portions from different scripture in order to craft your prayer. You will be able to keep yourself in faith by incorporating thanksgiving and praise into your lifestyle on a regular basis.

Finally, I want to share some of the discoveries we

made while we travelled through the rugged terrain that is prayer. It's easy to start with a lot of excitement. But it's not how you start that determines your success; it's how you continue. It's easy to become discouraged and frustrated in prayer. After all what makes anyone think the God of the universe is going to hear and answer prayer?

After you have asked God to help your children, to bless them and save them what else can you do? How can you be sure that your prayer is being heard, let alone being answered? The following is a list of some of the things that may lead to a more effective prayer life.

(1)   God is looking for partners (sons and daughters) who through prayer will help accomplish His will on the earth

(2)   God desires those who will pray *with* Him and not just *to* Him.

(3)   God desires that prayer be a dialogue not a monologue

(4)   God has already supplied the "script" for us to pray from. His Word contains His thoughts and desires as well as the many promises concerning what He will do for us.

(5)   We need to listen as well as speak. This is a partnership. What He has to say to us is always more important then what we have to say to Him. (Ecclesiastes 5:1-2)

(6)   It is easier to pray with others who are like-minded than to pray alone. Usually 2-3 others works best. Ecclesiastes 4:9-12; Matthew 18:19-20)

(7)   Having a set time and place of prayer helps to maintain the routine.

(8)   Be honest when communicating with God. It is pointless to try to hide anything from the One who sees and knows all things. Also, He is not impressed with fancy words or forms. (Matthew 6:7-13)

(9)   You must continue to believe what God's Word says. Ignore what you see and hear in the physical world and exercise the eyes of faith. (2 Corinthians 5:7)

(10)   Do not be discouraged if things seem to get worse before they get better. Remember the effect of the famine in the account of the prodigal son. (Luke 15:11-32)

(11)   Perseverance is the key to obtaining most things in the Kingdom of God. (Luke 8:15; James 1:2-4)

(12)   Remember that God loves your children more than you do. He sent His Son to die for them so they may be saved. (John 3:16)

AFTERWORD

It is almost bizarre how closely the trajectory of Nate's life followed his father's. They were products of somewhat dysfunctional homes, so some similarity it to be expected. But the parallels are striking. Both became involved with drugs when they were young, although Nate never became addicted. Each fathered a child while still a teen-ager. They followed nearly identical paths through the justice system landing in a maximum-security detention facility in their home state having been charged with basically the same felonies. It was in prison where each man came to the end of himself and surrendered to God.

In a marvelous picture of God's reckless love and unbounded grace, both Nate and Bill are involved in ministry to ex-offenders and recovering addicts. They are tackling the problem of recidivism from the outside and inside. As of this writing, both are going back to prison – this time through the auspices of Prison Fellowship – to teach and encourage currently incarcerated men what they have learned about the need for a biblical faith and a human support system when they are eventually released.

On the outside, Bill and Nate are involved in a reentry and recovery ministry called Fresh Coast Alliance in Muskegon, Michigan. Nate shares his story of being lost and found with anyone who will listen as he serves as a point person for Fresh Coast. Bill actively mentors participants and holds regular Bible studies for anyone interested in making better choices. Bill and Nate both serve as teaching pastors at Kingdom Life Church in Muskegon, a place that has intentionally opened its doors to returning citizens and recovering addicts.

Both men have travelled the dark road of sin and despair. They now bring the promise of light and hope to men and women who have fallen into the darkness they know so well. They speak with a knowing voice of God's unmerited grace and unending love toward all the prodigals who have run away. It is their passion to be the earthly father figure who runs to meet the wayward children when they come to the end of themselves and seek a better way. This similarity of life and purpose is the most wonderful to behold.

In case you missed it, Bill and Nate's purpose in telling their story is to encourage all who find themselves in a situation at the end of their rope. The moral of their story is that prayer does indeed change things. As Bill reminds us all, our God a god of the impossible. He admonishes us with the

Apostle Paul, "So let's not allow ourselves to get fatigued doing good. At the right time we will harvest a good crop if we don't give up or quit." (Galatians 6:9 MSG)

In His Service, Clair Verway

53400098R00039

Made in the
USA
Lexington, KY